Parenting Letters

40 original letters

responsibility · bickering · chores · bullies · I love you · comfort
tolerance · having fun · making choices · sorry I yelled at you
school grades · the perfect kid · setting limits · shopping
arguing · I'm not perfect · helping out · siblings · values · family
grief · you're on the team · life skills · growing up · health
communication · meals · practicing · behavior · hugs and kisses
let's talk · stress · coping skills · divorce · trust · family outings
nutrition · humor · teenagers · appreciation · breaking the rules
call home · relationships · hello from camp · first day of school

Published by LDF Publishing Inc 2001

First printing

ISBN 0-9696427-8-4

Published in Canada in 2001 by

LDF Publishing Inc
P.O. Box 45
Port Perry, ON
Canada L9L 1A2
(905) 985-9990
1-877-492-6845
info@ldfpublishing.com
www.parentingletters.com

Cover design by Raymond Gubala
Letter design by Maracle Press Ltd
Inside page design by LDF Publishing Inc

Printed in Canada by Maracle Press Ltd

To our children

Meg

Michael

Daniel

Luke

Why Letters?

"What Did You Say?"

We all know that talking to our children isn't always effective. With the best of intentions, we try to say the right words, use the right tone, find the right time - and even then, our message doesn't always get through. And so we try again. And probably again. And pretty soon we're on the brink of nagging. And by that time, they've often tuned us out.

And we wonder how we can handle the situation better next time.

Put it in Writing

As parents often do, we talked about our children when we got together. We shared parenting stories: what worked and what didn't. And we usually got around to discussing why our kids didn't "hear" what we were saying.

We tried to figure out how we could get them to consider our thoughts and ideas as they formed their values, opinions, and made their decisions. And we wanted to find more ways to encourage them and support them and show them we love them.

At some point, we took Susan's idea of writing letters to her children, and decided to write to our kids regularly.

I Read You Loud and Clear

And so we began leaving letters for them on their pillows or tucked in their backpacks. And before long we saw that writing to them worked. Our kids took time to think about the ideas we presented to them. And they did seem to better understand our point of view. Even if they didn't agree with us, they had another way of thinking about a situation. We even managed to see the funny side of things together. And with some time to think, their reaction to us softened.

Just as important, they could re-read the letters the way a child reads a favorite story over and over again. We wanted these letters to be something our children would want to keep. And they did treasure and keep many of them.

We'd discovered another way to communicate with our children.
And so we thought other parents could benefit from what we'd learned.

About the Letters

How to Use the Letters
These letters are intended to give you another way to talk to your child about the things that matter.

They can be given on special occasions or when your child needs a hug, similar to a greeting card.

For everyday situations, we've found it most effective to leave a letter where your child will easily find it - maybe on their desk, at their place at the table, or on their favorite living room chair. Or you could post the letter on the fridge. Or tape it to their door. Or leave it anywhere else you think of.

After your child has read it, you'll have a starting point where you can both present your thoughts and feelings, if the topic requires further discussion. Or maybe nothing further needs to be said...

For younger children, you might sit down and read the letter to them, just as you would a story. You can then talk about it together, explain what it means to you, and ask them what they got out of it.

Subject Matter
Many of the letters address a wide range of parenting issues and everyday situations, while others were written to give love, encouragement and support.

Age Range
Parenting letters are designed for all children of reading age, from 7 or 8 right up to the teenage years.

Gender: His and Hers
Most of the letters are written for any child, male or female. But where the content requires a letter to be gender specific, we've included two versions: one for a son and one for a daughter.

Tear Them Out!
The letters are perforated for easy use - just fold along the perforation, tear them out, sign them, and they're ready to give.

It matters how we talk to our children.

Of course, from time to time we all say things we wish we hadn't. Much as we try, we're only human.

But over the long haul, in the big picture, how we talk to them matters.

It matters because they matter. And they need to know that. But when we're distracted by the demands of everyday life or caught up in the emotion of the moment, we may cloud the message we want most to give our children: we love them and we cherish them.

In fact, I believe that's the only message we really need to get across.

I'm not too sure the rest makes much difference. It's probably not important whether we're strict or lenient, expressive or reserved, structured or laid back. As long as our kids know that at the heart of it all lies the unmistakable and consistent message "I love you", I believe they'll be okay.

These letters tell our children they're loved in 40 different ways. Whether we're talking about arguing, making choices, calling home, or coping with a tough situation, we're really saying we love them. The more ways we can express that, the stronger and clearer the message.

They need to hear it. So we need to say it. Every chance we get.

Lisa Fraser

My mother used to say,

> " A dog barking
> or a mother talking
> is the same thing. "

She was describing how our children tune us out and don't really hear what we're trying to say to them.

Of course, at the time, I would mirror her exasperation and reply, "I *am* listening", and I often could even recite word for word what she had said. But I wasn't listening - because I was disregarding her words. Her experience obviously didn't apply to me. I knew it all. Her love was, at best, taken for granted, at worst, actually a burden.

Being a mother didn't come naturally to me. I read the latest psychology books. I considered every opinion from the pros and cons of breast feeding to the pros and cons of giving an allowance. I struggled with every decision from bed time to how much TV to whether they might still have dessert if they couldn't finish their mashed potatoes. I made many mistakes along the way and would do many things differently if only I had the chance to have my children all over again. But somehow we all muddled through and they grew up and somehow became wonderful people.

At some point, I began writing letters to them. Hopefully a letter which they could re-read slowly would better sink in than my endless lecturing or nagging. Hopefully a letter would make up for my inability to say the right thing at the right time. Hopefully, a letter could explain what I'm doing and why.

Now that I'm over 50 years old, I'm beginning to understand what my mother went through. Hopefully with these letters, I won't have to wait until my kids are 50 before they understand me.

Susan Schulman

Table of Contents

The Letters

Dear

Congratulations! You're on the team!
I'm really happy for you.

Whether you win or not is secondary to me.
Most important is that you love the sport and
you enjoy playing it.

And anyway, I'm already proud of you.

I'm proud of your effort,
the hours you put in practicing,
the commitment you made to your team,
and for striving to be your best.

Of course, if your team does win,
there'll be another great reason to celebrate.

But you're already a winner in my book.

Love,

www.parentingletters.com

Dear

There's no such thing as a perfect person,
so don't ever think you've got to do
everything right. And anyway, that's
not the kind of kid I want. I don't want
a model child. I want someone who

laughs, crys,

gets mad, gets over it,

does some things well, does other things
poorly,

works hard, lays around and does nothing,

leaves their things all over the house,
cleans up eventually,

tries hard at school, is goofy at recess,

makes mistakes, does their best to fix them.

I want you just the way you are.
And that's perfect to me.

Love,

www.parentingletters.com

My Top Ten List
What I Want You to Know About Life

10. Be gentle with people. Treat them the way you'd like them to treat you.

9. Keep your word. Be someone people can trust and count on.

8. Approach life with a sense of humor. Laugh a lot.

7. Follow your dreams. If you want something strongly enough, go for it. Keep working at it. You can do it.

6. Have the courage to be true to yourself and your values. Live your life according to what YOU think is right.

5. Don't give up. When things are tough, when life is difficult, keep on going. It WILL get better.

4. Take time to do what you love doing. Life is to enjoy.

3. Do what matters. Life doesn't last forever, so make sure you do what's important to you.

2. Life is a gift. Find something to appreciate in each day.

And the number one thing I want you to know:

1. You're an awesome, special, wonderful person, and my life is infinitely richer because you're in it.

Dear

I'm so sorry that I yelled at you like that,
and I want to apologize.

So often when a parent gets angry,
the kid thinks it's their fault. That's not always so.

Sometimes I'm in an awful mood,
I'm just looking for something to get mad at, and
you just happen to be there. But that's no excuse.
You don't deserve such harsh words from me.

Sometimes I have other things bothering me
and whatever you're doing is simply the last straw.
But that's no excuse for me blowing it out of
proportion. You're just a kid being a kid.

Sometimes we do get angry at each other.
That's part of being human. Kids are allowed to be
angry at their parents, too. But being angry does
NOT give me the right to treat you poorly.

If anyone else talked to you the way I did
(maybe a teacher or another parent or a
babysitter) I'd never let THEM get away with it.
I shouldn't have talked to you that way myself.

What makes me feel the worst
is that I love you so much, and I sure didn't
treat you like the cherished child you are.
I'm sorry. And I love you.

Love,

www.parentingletters.com

"We're NOT arguing!"

Dear

I'm trying to remember if I was like that at your age, always trying to have the last word, tossing out insults like they don't matter. Maybe I was, maybe all kids communicate like that, maybe you're NOT arguing.

It sure sounds awful to me, though.
And it makes it impossible for me to be part of the conversation.

Even if you think you're not hurting the other person's feelings,
isn't there a better way of expressing yourself?
How about if YOU simply don't answer instead of telling the other person to shut up?
Why can't you simply disagree instead of calling the other person stupid?
Can't you voice your own opinion without belittling the other person for theirs?

People will pay more attention and will respect you more that way.
They may actually listen to what you're saying.
And that's what you ultimately want, isn't it?

Love,

www.parentingletters.com

Dear

I don't care what grades you get.

Yes, you read that right.

What matters to me is your effort.

Success in life doesn't depend solely on your grades, although it seems that way while you're in school. When you're out in the working world, people won't ask you what you got on your 10th grade math test. Although...the better you do at school, the more options you create for yourself. But grades aren't what matter most.

One very important thing you'll do to ensure success throughout your life is to have a solid work ethic. The most successful people are the ones who get things done (on time!), and who put in the effort required to do a decent job. It's amazing how often things turn out well when you work at them and see them through to completion.

I realize that you won't necessarily work your hardest at all your homework, nor at every project you are assigned. But if I see you doing more than the bare minimum on your assignments, making sure you study for tests, not leaving your schoolwork to the last minute, I'll be satisfied.

And your grades will take care of themselves.

Love,

I can:

love and guide you

help you figure out
right from wrong

give you my best advice

emphasize kindness and
sharing

talk with you about what
makes a good friend

encourage you to build your
self worth

teach you about personal
safety

point out the dangers of
drugs, alcohol and smoking

help you set goals

stress integrity

love you no matter what

Love,

but it's your responsibility to:

make good decisions

do the right thing

decide when and how to use it

show caring and generosity to others

surround yourself with good people

stand up for yourself and believe in
yourself

keep yourself safe and avoid dangerous
situations

say no

work toward them

live integrity

you don't have to do anything for that.

www.parentingletters.com

Dear

How about you put down your video game controller and we'll go for a walk on the beach.
Let's gather the smoothest stones we can find, and I'll show you how to skip them across the water. We'll dig a huge hole in the sand, so big that you can sit in it.

How about you put your video on pause and we'll go out in the rain.
Let's gather some twigs and sail them like little boats down the gutter. We'll use our feet to build a dam out of sand, and then watch until the current washes it away.

How about you power down your computer game and we'll go outside and lie on the grass together.
Let's look up at the clouds and watch them drift by. We'll look for ships and airplanes and elephants in the cloud formations.

How about you turn off the TV and we'll go for a bike ride together.
Let's fold bits of cardboard and fasten them to our spokes with clothes pegs. We'll listen to the whirring, fluttering sound they make as we pedal hard and pick up speed.

How about you put your CD player on mute and we'll rake a huge pile of leaves that we can jump in.
Let's bury you until you're completely covered up. We'll notice the smell of autumn in the leaves and listen to them crunch under us as we roll in them.

How about it...?

Love,

Dear

Most children's stories have family homes where there are two parents, two or three children with at least one boy and one girl, and often a dog or a cat. But that's not the only kind of family there is.

Someone recently told me they thought their family was incomplete because they have only one parent. That's just not so - a family is complete, whatever it is. Would you think your family was incomplete if you had three more sisters but no brothers? What about kids who never knew their grandparents - would you say their family is incomplete? Of course not. A family is complete, however big or small it is.

A family home might be made up of just two people: one parent and one child. It might include your grandmother or your aunt or the man who lives downstairs or your nanny or your cousin or any combination of people - and in many cases, your beloved pet.

Did you know that in some countries, it's common to continue living in the home you grew up in? In these countries, after you're married, you bring your husband or wife home to live with you, and you all stay there and live together as a family, even after you have your own children.

Whoever makes up your family home, that's your complete family home.

Love,

"Settle down.
  ...That's enough.
  ...Would you please STOP!"

Dear

Adults don't do well with silly behavior. We're always telling kids to keep it down, act appropriately for their age, smarten up, be more mature....

But you know, I really do get a kick out of the goofy things you do. Lots of times I'm smiling on the inside, even when I'm telling you to stop what you're doing.

You probably wonder why, if I think you're funny, I don't just laugh along with you.

I guess it's because I've got to teach you where and when it's okay to behave like that. Even if you are comical, it may not be the right place or the right atmosphere for that kind of behavior. I'm probably afraid that if I laugh, you'll get too carried away, or you'll think it's okay to ham it up anywhere.

But maybe I just need to lighten up. Maybe at times I forget what it's like to be a kid. Being silly is part of the fun of being a kid. I can lose sight of that when I get caught up in being the responsible parent.

I need to laugh with you more often.

Love,

Dear

I'm so drained from arguing with you
about things that are for your own health:
what you eat,
when you sleep,
what clothes to wear when it's freezing outside,
what TV you can't watch.

I wonder how long you'd last if I just let you:
live on ice cream and chips,
stay up until you were exhausted,
go out in the snow without hat and mitts until
your ears and fingers froze off,
watch the X-files until you had nightmares!

Love,

www.parentingletters.com

Dear

The girl you saw with the blue hair, matching lipstick and — how
many studs in her nose did she have?

She's not weird or scary because she dresses like that.
Granted, you may not be used to her style. But she's a human
being, just like you. She's got a favorite dessert, a subject at
school she's good at, a season she likes best. There are movies
that make her cry, and memories that make her smile. Her
choice of dress doesn't tell you what kind of person she is.

And the homeless man we passed who was pushing the shopping
cart that held everything he owns?

He's just a person, too. He doesn't look like most other people
you know, and sometimes different can make you uncomfortable —
but he's only a guy whose life has been harder than most. For
whatever reason — maybe no job, maybe a job that didn't pay
enough, maybe even his choice — he lives on the street. But he,
too, has a song that reminds him of his first girlfriend, an
opinion on who's the greatest sports team, a favorite place to
eat, and possibly, a few regrets.

As you see more of the world, you'll discover more
and more people with lifestyles that are different from yours.

But you won't know what kind of person they are until you get to
know them.

Love,

www.parentingletters.com

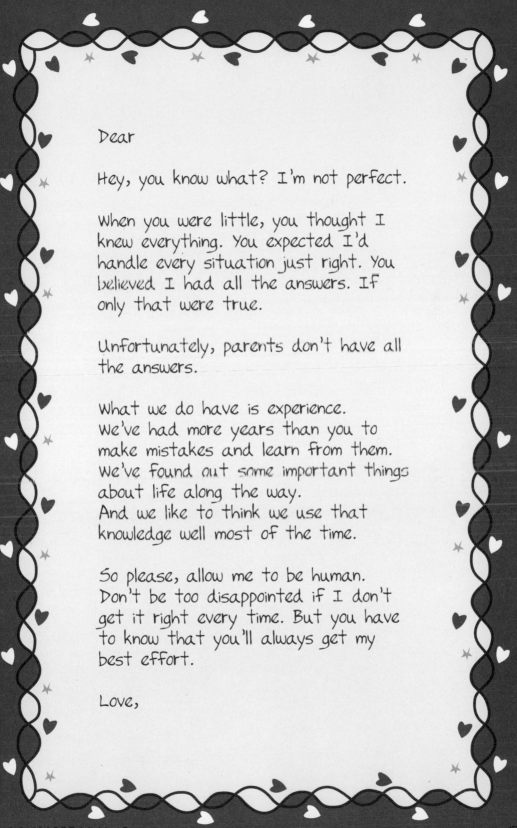

Dear

Hey, you know what? I'm not perfect.

When you were little, you thought I knew everything. You expected I'd handle every situation just right. You believed I had all the answers. If only that were true.

Unfortunately, parents don't have all the answers.

What we do have is experience. We've had more years than you to make mistakes and learn from them. We've found out some important things about life along the way. And we like to think we use that knowledge well most of the time.

So please, allow me to be human. Don't be too disappointed if I don't get it right every time. But you have to know that you'll always get my best effort.

Love,

Dear

Sometimes you're a wall.

I try so hard to reach you,
but when you answer, it doesn't come from you,
it comes from a wall in front of you.
Have I gotten through, or have my words just bounced off that wall?

Meaningless, acceptable, uncommitted answers
are what we encounter in casual polite company.
This is designed not to encourage openness,
but to close it off and guard against it.
Let's not reduce our relationship to that.
Let's not just have "safe" topics.

Sometimes people get so good at talking
from behind their wall, they forget who they really are.
Or they feel terribly alone and don't even know it.

Have I been so critical, so judgmental, that such a wall
was necessary with me?

Please remind me when I'm being too hard on you.
But don't close down.

Love,

www.parentingletters.com

Dear

I wish I could take your hurt away.

I love you so much that I'd gladly take on your pain myself if that would spare you what you're going through.

When you were younger, I often COULD make things better. I could mend your world by sewing up the tear in your beloved teddy bear. I could take away your tears with an ice cream cone or a trip to the park. I could repair the damage by gluing all the pieces together again. But this time, I can't make it all better. And there's nothing I wish I could do more.

There's only one thing I CAN do. I can be with you.

I can be with you, when it feels like you're all alone and no one understands. You haven't lost everything or everyone, although it may feel like it right now.

And I'll hold you through it, whenever and for however long you need me to.

Love,

Dear

The new school year begins again soon.
You probably have a lot of mixed feelings.

Summer's over, and in some ways you
wish you never had to return to school.
But then again, it'll be good to see all
of your friends again.

You wonder what your new teacher will
be like and you hope you'll be able to
keep up with the school work. But then
again, you worried about that last year
and it turned out okay.

Are you feeling unsettled by it all? New
situations can do that to you. But then
again, some new things aren't half bad -
you get to shop for new clothes and use
your new binders and backpack.

You have to get used to a daily routine
again, one which includes the tough stuff
like getting up on time. But then again,
the routine also includes good stuff like
music, phys ed, recess, class trips, and
weekends.

As we move into September, there's a
lot to look forward to. Let's make it a
great year.

Love,

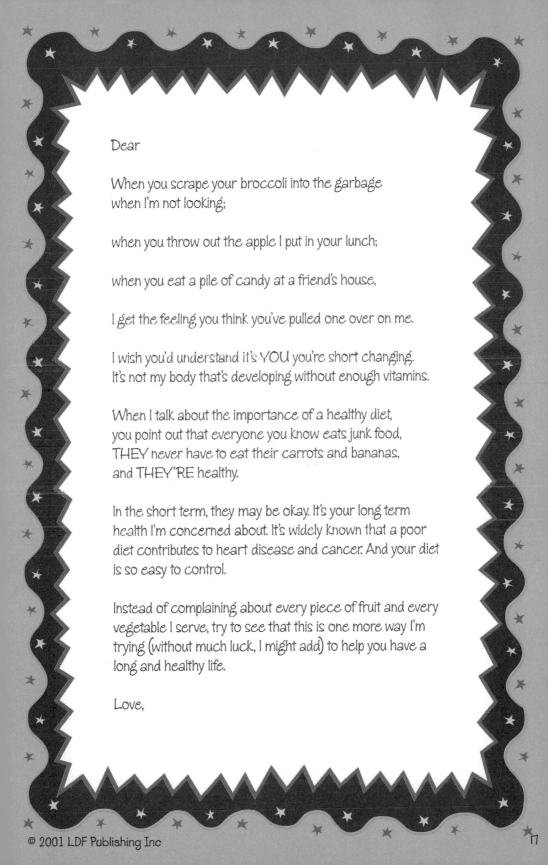

Dear

When you scrape your broccoli into the garbage
when I'm not looking;

when you throw out the apple I put in your lunch;

when you eat a pile of candy at a friend's house,

I get the feeling you think you've pulled one over on me.

I wish you'd understand it's YOU you're short changing.
It's not my body that's developing without enough vitamins.

When I talk about the importance of a healthy diet,
you point out that everyone you know eats junk food,
THEY never have to eat their carrots and bananas,
and THEY'RE healthy.

In the short term, they may be okay. It's your long term
health I'm concerned about. It's widely known that a poor
diet contributes to heart disease and cancer. And your diet
is so easy to control.

Instead of complaining about every piece of fruit and every
vegetable I serve, try to see that this is one more way I'm
trying (without much luck, I might add) to help you have a
long and healthy life.

Love,

www.parentingletters.com

"Why can't I? You're not my boss."

Dear

If you were walking in front of a moving train
and I yelled at you and pushed you hard, I think you WOULD appreciate my help.
You'd easily agree that it wasn't the appropriate time to DISCUSS
whether you should move or not.

The trouble is, I push you so soon that you never even believe there WAS a train,
and you get mad at me for pushing.
You think that I overreact, that I'm totally unreasonable,
you don't see the point to my rules and my caution.
Well, maybe at your age you're supposed to think you're invincible.

But if you would only remember
that even at my most unreasonable moments, I'm acting that way because
I love you and want to protect you from all harm, even though I know that's impossible.
I do understand that there aren't that many moving trains.
And I CAN tell the difference between a train and a mosquito (even though I might
not act like there's any difference).
The trouble is I want to protect you from even a mosquito.

I worry that you can't yet tell the difference, and that you never even see the trains.
I don't want you to get hit by one before you learn to look out for them.
It's hard for me to let you learn from your own experiences.

You think I'm making too big a deal about every little thing.
I do understand that I'm not your boss.
But don't reject me for trying to take care of you. It's my nature to protect you,
just as it's your nature to throw off that protection.
It's my nature to want to keep you totally safe,
just as it's your nature to assume you can take care of yourself.

Love,

www.parentingletters.com

Dear

You're such a neat person.
I'm so glad you're my kid.

Just think,
over your whole lifetime, and
of all the people in the world,
only a few will get to know you
as well as I will.

I feel very privileged to be
one of those people.

Love,

www.parentingletters.com

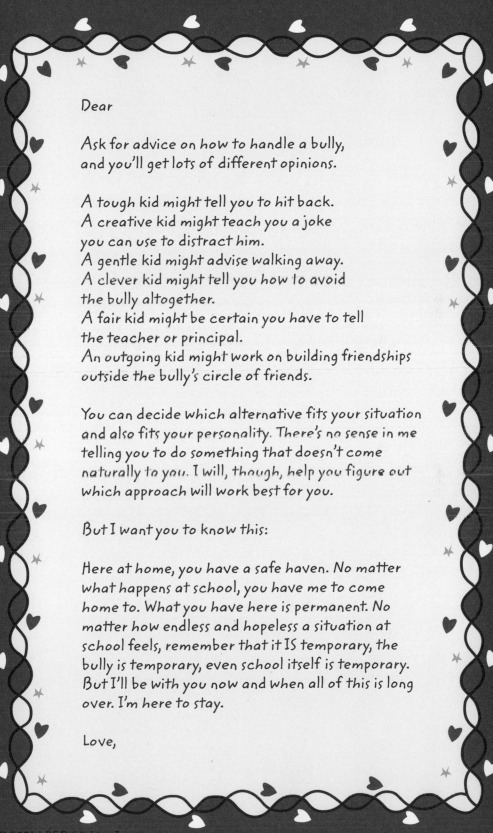

Dear

Ask for advice on how to handle a bully,
and you'll get lots of different opinions.

A tough kid might tell you to hit back.
A creative kid might teach you a joke
you can use to distract him.
A gentle kid might advise walking away.
A clever kid might tell you how to avoid
the bully altogether.
A fair kid might be certain you have to tell
the teacher or principal.
An outgoing kid might work on building friendships
outside the bully's circle of friends.

You can decide which alternative fits your situation
and also fits your personality. There's no sense in me
telling you to do something that doesn't come
naturally to you. I will, though, help you figure out
which approach will work best for you.

But I want you to know this:

Here at home, you have a safe haven. No matter
what happens at school, you have me to come
home to. What you have here is permanent. No
matter how endless and hopeless a situation at
school feels, remember that it IS temporary, the
bully is temporary, even school itself is temporary.
But I'll be with you now and when all of this is long
over. I'm here to stay.

Love,

www.parentingletters.com

Dear

You MUST know that no matter what, I'll love you. So if you get into trouble, if you didn't obey my rules, I'll still be there to rescue you. But I'll be mad.

If, against my rules, you don't wear your wrist guards when you're roller blading, I'll be there to put the ice on if you fall and sprain your wrist. But I'll be mad and I might nag about safety and about doing what I say.

If, against my rules, you drink too much, PLEASE call me when you need a ride home. But all the way, I'll be mad and I might nag about drinking and about doing what I say.

I want you to understand that I just love you so much. And you're just gonna have to put up with me - sometimes I just won't keep quiet.

Love,

Dear

        O Mom   O Dad   O _____

Hello from camp. How is everybody at home?

My counsellor is   O nice.   O a monster.

So far, I am   O having a great fantastic wonderful time.
    O having a good time.
    O not having a good time.

The weather here is mostly
    O sunny.   O cloudy.   O raining.

The food here is   O OK.   O bad.   O rotten.

O I have made a new friend whose name is _____.

O In the water, for the first time I was able to _____.

O I'm making a   O bracelet
    O keychain
    O necklace
    O other: _____.

Something else I want to tell you about:

_____

_____

Well, that's all I can think of to tell you now.

From your loving   O daughter O son _____.

Dear

Let's talk.

A good conversation
allows people to express themselves openly,
and to trusl
that they won't be shot down for their opinions or their preferences.
I want to have that openness with you. Please let me in
to your world.

Those glib answers are a tool that might be useful
when you're older, in business or in certain social situations.
I hope you won't need it very often with best friends or with your spouse,
and I wish you wouldn't use it with me.

Let's have conversations
where we can honestly interchange ideas and feelings.

I know there's a person inside you who feels deeply
and who understands a lot.
Please be that person with me.

Love,

www.parentingletters.com

Dear

You just can't believe he's really not alive. I know.
Only recently you were playing together, laughing together.
And now you just can't believe that you'll never see him again
in real life.

But it's good to remember the fun you had together,
even though remembering makes you sad too.
It's good to remember his laugh and his games and the twinkle
in his eyes and all the fun you had together.

It's also good to remember what you learned from him.
Not just the sort of things you might learn in school,
but also things about life. So remember him.
Remember what you learned from him about what is really important,
about behavior, about friendships,
about being kind and generous and strong.
It's good to talk about him.
Even though talking might make you sad too because you miss him.
Talk about what he taught you and what he showed you.

He also contributed things to the world didn't he. He made the
world a better place.
He was a good person and people liked him and it's good to think of
those things. It's good to be able to remember him in these ways
and to talk about him.
If you remember the joy that he brought, you'll be able to smile
through your tears.

Love,

Dear

You just can't believe she's really not alive. I know.
Only recently you were playing together, laughing together.
And now you just can't believe that you'll never see her again
in real life.

But it's good to remember the fun you had together,
even though remembering makes you sad too.
It's good to remember her laugh and her games and the twinkle
in her eyes and all the fun you had together.

It's also good to remember what you learned from her.
Not just the sort of things you might learn in school,
but also things about life. So remember her.
Remember what you learned from her about what is really important,
about behavior, about friendships,
about being kind and generous and strong.
It's good to talk about her.
Even though talking might make you sad too because you miss her.
Talk about what she taught you and what she showed you.

She also contributed things to the world didn't she. She made the
world a better place.
She was a good person and people liked her and it's good to think of
those things. It's good to be able to remember her in these ways
and to talk about her.
If you remember the joy that she brought, you'll be able to smile
through your tears.

Love,

www.parentingletters.com

Dear

I trust you.

Each time you keep your word, do what you said you'd do, use good judgement, you solidify that trust.

Trust CAN be shaken, though. As soon as you lie to someone, mislead them, don't keep your word, they wonder what you'll do next time. Once you give them reason to doubt you, you have to prove yourself a number of times before you rebuild that trust.

You may come to a time where you think it's better to not tell me something, or maybe hide something from me...but I want to assure you that you can always tell me what you're doing. You may think that you're avoiding a conflict, and yes, we may disagree in the short term - but as long as we're open about things, our long term trust will remain intact. And I'll be much more likely to let you do things. And our relationship will be that much stronger.

Love,

www.parentingletters.com

"Why NOT? WHY can't I?
Give me ONE good reason!
I said a GOOD reason!"

Dear

Didn't I already say NO?
Why do you keep asking me?

I know why:
You've learned that if you bug me enough,
I sometimes change my mind.

You think it's your persistent bugging
that wears me down?
It upsets me all right,
and it angers me that you're continually challenging me.
But you have no IDEA what goes through my head.

You want to watch just one more program, stay up later, not wear your boots,
eat 3 chocolate bars for lunch, impulse-buy something.

One of my voices says,
"It's such a little thing, and it will make her happy. What real harm can it do?

Another of my voices says,
"She's got to learn. She shouldn't think that she can have everything she wants.
It's not good for her, and it won't be healthy in the long run."

Another of my voices says,
"What if, (God forbid!) there ISN'T any long run? Anything can happen! How
can I deny her these little pleasures? Nobody knows what the future holds!

I have other voices too. The one thing in common is my concern for you: your
safety, your happiness, your well-being. My answers to you reflect whichever is
the loudest voice at the time.

Love,

www.parentingletters.com

"Why NOT? WHY can't I?
Give me ONE good reason!
I said a GOOD reason!"

Dear

Didn't I already say NO?
Why do you keep asking me?

I know why:
You've learned that if you bug me enough,
I sometimes change my mind.

You think it's your persistent bugging
that wears me down?
It upsets me all right,
and it angers me that you're continually challenging me.
But you have no IDEA what goes through my head.

You want to watch just one more program, stay up later, not wear your boots,
eat 3 chocolate bars for lunch, impulse-buy something.

One of my voices says,
"It's such a little thing, and it will make him happy. What real harm can it do?

Another of my voices says,
"He's got to learn. He shouldn't think that he can have everything he wants.
It's not good for him, and it won't be healthy in the long run."

Another of my voices says,
"What if, (God forbid!) there ISN'T any long run? Anything can happen! How
can I deny him these little pleasures? Nobody knows what the future holds!

I have other voices too. The one thing in common is my concern for you: your
safety, your happiness, your well-being. My answers to you reflect whichever is
the loudest voice at the time.

Love,

Dear

What is a family?

A family is more than just a bunch of people who live together in the same building. A family is more than an arrangement for shared accommodation.

Being in a family means that every once in a while we hang out together. Maybe just by all having at least one meal together each day. Maybe just by sitting around in the living room and talking together for awhile.

Being part of a family also means we mention when we're going out and where we're going and maybe when we think we'll be back and maybe even how we can be reached.

Being part of a family also means that we cover for each other. If one kid has a broken ankle then the other kid walks the dog. If one kid is very late for school then the other kid helps make lunch. We don't start arguing about whose job it is or whether it's fair. We're in this together.

I would really like us to be more of a family.

Love,

www.parentingletters.com

My Dearest   ○ Mother   ○ Father   ○ _____ :
(Please check all that apply and fill in the blanks.)

I'm leaving now, and the time is: _____.

○ I have gone to a friend's house.
                Their name is

                _____

                Their address and phone number is

                _____

○ I'm meeting friend(s)
                Here are their names

                _____

                _____.

                This is where we're going

                _____

I'll call you when I get there and let you know when I'm leaving.

I expect to be home by approximately this time: _____.

I understand that you'd like this information because:

    ○ you care about me and want to be sure I'm okay.
    ○ you think I can't take care of myself (but I can!).
    ○ you need to know how to reach me.
    ○ you worry too much and this will help.
    ○ I don't do a good job of keeping you informed and
      maybe this will work.

From your

○ loving   ○ adoring   ○ grateful   ○ devoted

○ son   ○ daughter

                Signed _____.

Dear

What happened to the little girl who used to hold my hand
oh so tightly when we walked together?
Where's the little girl who jumped into my arms
as soon as I got in the door?
Where's the child who looked up at me with complete trust
in her huge wide-open eyes?
I miss the little girl who snuggled up to me
for a bedtime story,
who fell asleep in my arms,
who confided in me,
and came to me for comfort.

I know your independence now is healthy growing up.
I can joke with other parents of teenagers about what
you've all turned into.
We console ourselves by telling ourselves you'll understand us
when you have children of your own.

But in my heart, I also know that too often I was too strict
or too inconsistent or too busy or too harsh or too critical.
And I pray that somehow we can be close again.

Love,

www.parentingletters.com

Dear

What happened to the little boy who used to hold my hand
oh so tightly when we walked together?
Where's the little boy who jumped into my arms
as soon as I got in the door?
Where's the child who looked up at me with complete trust
in his huge wide-open eyes?
I miss the little boy who snuggled up to me
for a bedtime story,
who fell asleep in my arms,
who confided in me,
and came to me for comfort.

I know your independence now is healthy growing up.
I can joke with other parents of teenagers about what
you've all turned into.
We console ourselves by telling ourselves you'll understand us
when you have children of your own.

But in my heart, I also know that too often I was too strict
or too inconsistent or too busy or too harsh or too critical.
And I pray that somehow we can be close again.

Love,

Dear

In one way or another,
we're always emphasizing how important it is to be happy.

We tell you that we just want you to be happy.
Storybooks usually have a happy ending.
Kids' movies all work out in the end.
Even TV commercials promise a good life, if only you buy the right things.

But maybe that gives you the message that life should be storybook happy.
Maybe that leads you to think that bad things won't and shouldn't happen.
Maybe we're setting you up to have false expectations about life.

But tough times DO happen. Life is made up of BOTH good and bad.
Nobody gets away without difficult chapters in their life.
We all experience them at one time or another.

I guess I'm saying all this because when something bad happens,
I don't want you to focus on the unfairness of it.
Some people get stuck in feeling ripped off,
instead of doing what they can to work through it.

I want you to always remember that life is good,
even if it IS difficult at times.
That doesn't mean that life is always happy, but it's still good.
And valuable. And worth your best effort.

Love,

Dear

People walk their dogs in the park. Some mornings they find broken glass all over the ground. The dog owners carefully pick up the sharp pieces of glass. It's not fair that they have to do that. But nobody wants a dog to cut its paws. Sometimes you have to do something just because it needs to be done — not because it's your job.

I know it's not your job to put away things that you haven't even used, but they still have to be put away. And who wants to clear someone else's dirty plate off the table? Sometimes I ask you simply because you're nearby and it would be helpful. I don't pick on you, and I don't always ask just you to do these things, and I'm not sitting around at these times — I'm doing things too. So please don't give me such a hard time when I ask you to help.

Love,

www.parentingletters.com

Dear

I'd like to introduce you to a few household objects I don't believe you're familiar with:

This is a toothpaste tube lid. It was designed to keep toothpaste from drying out and clogging up the opening of the toothpaste tube. You screw it back on after you squeeze toothpaste onto your brush. If you use it regularly, you'll find you can get toothpaste out of a tube that is more than a few days old.

 This is a toilet flusher. It's actually a little lever. After you've used the facilities, you push the lever down, and the toilet flushes. It leaves the toilet clean and ready for the next person. It's considered good manners to use it.

This is a towel rack. I think you may have mistaken the bathroom floor for this object. After you've showered or taken a bath, you hang the wet towels on it so they can dry out. There are two benefits to using it: (1) you'll have a dry towel for your next bath or shower, and (2) the smell of mildew won't take over the house.

 You're already somewhat familiar with the light switch. You've learned to turn it on, but I thought you should know that it has an "off" position, too. As you're leaving a room, you flip the switch downward to turn off the light. There's a bonus when you use this mechanism to its full capacity: we save a bit of money on our electric bill every single time you turn a light off.

This is a kitchen sink. It's a multi-purpose device: it's the holding place for dirty dishes (vs. the kitchen table or your bedroom floor), and it's also where dishes get washed. If you can't find a clean glass or plate, fill the sink with hot water, add dish soap, and wash whatever kitchen item you need at the time.

If you come across any further household articles that require clarification, please feel free to ask.

Love,

Dear

I don't know what's bothering you,
but taking it out on me won't help. I'll end up
feeling rotten, too, and for what reason?
I haven't done anything to you.

But hey –

if you're hurt, I'll talk with you about it.

If you're stressed out,
I'll help you find a way to ease the pressure.

If you're angry, I'll listen to you.

If you're tired, for gosh sakes, get some rest.

You have the right to feel lousy.
But as awful as you may feel, you DON'T
have the right to behave any way you want.

Let's find a way to deal with this situation
without causing any more hurt than is
already there.

Love,

Dear

Grocery shopping
takes so much time,
and the line ups are the worst!

But when I take you shopping with me,
I enjoy it.

When you run to check the pictures on the
cereal boxes,
when you pick out the best apples for me,
even when you're pleading with me for the
candy you can't have,
I have as much fun
as spending the afternoon at the park.

You turn an every day chore into
a fun outing,
and best of all,
I get a chance to spend time with you.

Love,

www.parentingletters.com

Dear

When you get a present for someone,
it's fun, isn't it, to pick something out that you hope they'll like,
to watch them smile when they open it,
maybe even to play together with that present.

You didn't get that present just to hear them say "thank you",
but it's still nice when they do say it.
And it's nice to see that they're happy with your gift.

It's the same when I do things for you.
I want to do things for you. I like doing things for you.
You don't have to thank me all the time.
But it still would be so nice if you acknowledged what I do.

How would you feel if your friend just grabbed the present and ignored you?
That's how I feel sometimes.
How would you feel if your friend just grabbed the present and then
asked you what else you brought?
That's how I feel too sometimes.

Love,

www.parentingletters.com

You have two choices for dinner:

take it
or leave it.

36

www.parentingletters.com

Dear

You've heard us say, often enough,
that this should be the best time of your life.
"You have your youthful energy, no responsibilities,
everything is taken care of for you,
and all you have to do is learn things.
Why aren't you appreciative?"

I've been thinking that this is probably
one of the most difficult times of your life.

You have to explain what you're doing all the time,
ask for permission to go anywhere,
then you have to ask for a ride,
then you have to ask for money.

You have to defend the clothes you wear,
the music you listen to,
the friends you choose,
the way you are.

You feel old enough to run your own life,
old enough to have adult feelings,
and then are told you AREN'T old enough.

You want to be independent,
but there are times you still need me,
even though that's hard to admit.

I remember what it's like to be in your shoes.
It's not easy.

Love,

Dear

You don't feel like practicing, I can see that. It's boring, you have better things to spend your time on... and mastering a new concept can be difficult. But there's no shortcut to learning.

When you were learning how to walk, talk, read, write, run, ride your bike, whatever - you learned by doing it over and over again until you knew how. You didn't just wake up one day and decide you were going to walk. You kept at it until you could do it.

A pro basketball player doesn't show up for a game automatically knowing how to shoot a 3-pointer.

A ballerina doesn't prance onto the stage knowing how to do a pirouette.

A musician doesn't know how to play a concerto simply by walking on stage. Even a musician who improvises spends hours practicing chords behind the scenes.

They make it look easy, but they've all spent years practicing their craft. They weren't born with that level of skill. They've worked and worked and worked at it, many times practicing when they didn't feel like it. That's how they became so good.

No one's asking you to become a world class performer. But you can't learn just by showing up at lessons or games. That's why you have to practice.

Love,

Dear

I can't stand it when you guys bicker.

Of course, the noise and commotion make me crazy.
But that's not the worst of it -
the reason it bothers me goes far beyond the noise.

Arguing and quarrelling are not my idea of what a family is all
about. I envision us looking out for each other,
supporting and encouraging each other,
not trying to hurt each other with unkind words.
It's hard to hear you guys talk to each other the way you do
when you're fighting.

You never speak to your friends that way.
Doesn't your family deserve the best of you, too?
Just because you think they'll always be there doesn't mean
you can treat them any way you like.
And I hope that YOU guys will be close, lifelong friends,
in it together, to celebrate the good times
and help each other through the tough times.

So please try to use care, love and respect
when you deal with each other. You have a special relationship.
I hope you'll eventually see how important you really are
to each other.

Love,

Dear

Everyone will tell you (and it IS completely true),
that we both still love you and always will,
that our divorce has nothing to do with you and is not your fault, and
we can stop loving each other but we'll never stop loving our children.

But what they don't tell you is how life will change.
Obviously our living arrangements will change.
But something else happens when parents get divorced.
Our relationship with you changes.

Sometimes we'll talk to you like you're a close friend,
asking your opinions about adult things,
confiding our own feelings to you.
You might even think that's a good change, but it's not always.
I'll try to not be that way, but sometimes it just happens.
No matter how old you are, you're still my child, not just my buddy.

There will be more chores. I'll be asking you to help me more than ever.

We might be more impatient with you. Or just more tired.

You are a wonderful, unique person.
Still, naturally, you also have some of both of us in you.
And as much as we love you, sometimes we see the other parent in you.
There's nothing wrong with that,
but it might bother us more than it should.
We might say, you're acting just like your father/mother.
There's no reason for us to be angry about that, but we still might be.

cont'd on next page...

www.parentingletters.com

cont'd. from previous page....

It's very difficult for one parent to be everything.
I feel it's more important than ever
to be a strict boss and keep the rules because when you're with me,
there is no other boss anymore.
But at the same time, I want to love you to pieces more than ever,
because when we're alone there's no one else for that either.
So there will be more extremes —
sometimes I'll be too easy and sometimes I'll be too tough.

I'll do my best. And I know you'll do your best to understand.

Love,

We welcome your suggestions:

If you have an idea or a topic you think would make a good letter, please let us know and we'll consider including it in a future edition.

If you have any suggestions, or if you'd like to purchase additional copies of Parenting Letters, you can reach us at:

Parenting Letters
LDF Publishing Inc.
P.O. Box 45, Port Perry
Ontario, Canada L9L 1A2

(905) 985-9990
1-877-492-6845

or you can email us at: info@ldfpublishing.com

Please visit our website:

www.parentingletters.com